Start With Listening

Beginning Comprehension Practice

Patricia A. Dunkel
Department of Speech Communication
and
Center for English as a Second Language
The Pennsylvania State University

Christine Grady Gorder
Center for English as a Second Language
University of Arizona

HEINLE & HEINLE PUBLISHERS
A Division of Wadsworth, Inc.
Boston, Massachusetts 02116

Library of Congress Cataloging-in-Publication Data

Dunkel, Patricia.
  Start with listening.

  1. English language—Text-books for foreign speakers.
2. Listening—Problems, exercises, etc.   I. Gorder,
Christine Grady.   II. Title.
PE1128.D8274   1987   428.3'4   86-19180

Grateful acknowledgment is given for the use of the following photographs. p. 54, lower, right, Rafael
Millán; *p. 62, left,* Rafael Millán, *right,* Gary Cichowski, *Concord Journal,* Concord, MA 01742;
p. 67, left, Rafael Millán; *p. 74, left and middle,* U.S. Navy Photographs by Joc John Burplage, *right,*
Rafael Millán; *p. 85,* Margaret Grant; *p. 123,* Rafael Millán; *p. 138, top, left,* Ron Solomon,
Canadian Government Film & Video Centre, Ottowa, *bottom, right,* A. Sima, Canadian
Government Film & Video Centre, Ottowa; *p. 140, top, right,* Société de Transport de la
Communauté Urbaine de Montréal; *p. 146,* Rafael Millán.

Sponsoring Editor/James Brown
Project coordination/Maeve A. Cullinane
Interior and cover design/Carson Design
Illustration/Len Shalansky
Composition/Waldman Graphics
Printing/McNaughton & Gunn, Inc.

ISBN 0-8384-2820-7

Printed in the U.S.A.   First printing: March 1987
6321327   10

TABLE OF CONTENTS

Grammatical Structures	Expressions
Tense: simple present (verb BE affirmative);	In a minute
Yes/no questions;	Let's go.
Predicate adjectives;	Everything is in order.
Prepositional phrases	Flight 65 is ready to take off.
	Here it is.
	Here's your ticket.

Grammatical Structures	Expressions
Tense: simple present (verb BE affirmative);	He's from Boston.
Yes/no and Wh- questions;	Sarah is on the way to Harvard.
Predicate adjectives;	Can I help you?
Introductory form–There are.	It's nice to meet you.
Determiner (some)	Let me help you.
	Thanks a lot.

Grammatical Structures	**Expressions**
Tenses: simple present, present continuous (verb BE, affirmative and negative);	I'm fine.
Wh- questions;	What's new?
Other verbs (including have) third person singular;	Great!
Possessive pronoun (her);	Cristina is on the phone.
Frequency adverbs (often, sometimes, usually)	How about a movie?
	Too bad.

Grammatical Structures
Tenses: simple present, present
continuous (verb BE,
affirmative and negative);
Wh- questions;
Other verbs (including have)
third person singular;
Possessive pronoun (her);
Frequency adverbs (often,
sometimes, usually)

Expressions
I'm fine.
What's new?
Great!
Cristina is on the phone.
How about a movie?
Too bad.

Grammatical Structures
Tenses: simple present, present
continuous (verb BE,
affirmative and negative);
Other verbs (including have)
third person singular;
Possessive pronoun (his);
Predicate adjectives;
Introductory form–There is/There
are;
Frequency adverb (always);
Imperative (affirmative)

Expressions
It's crazy.
Come on!
What's the difference?
What a surprise!
He's driving me crazy.

Grammatical Structures	**Expressions**
Tenses: simple present, present continuous; Verb BE and other verbs (affirmative and negative, singular and plural); Predicate adjectives; Introductory form–There are; Frequency adverbs (always, never); Imperatives (affirmative and negative); Modals (can/can't)	Turn down the music. Oh, come on. Tony's father is standing in line. How's Mom doing? Think about it.

Grammatical Structures	**Expressions**
Tenses: simple present, present continuous; Verb BE and other verbs (affirmative and negative, singular and plural); Frequency adverbs; Imperatives, second person singular (affirmative and negative), first person plural (affirmative); Verbs (hate to, want to)	What a day! What would you like? I'll get it. Let's not cook tonight. Let's eat out. It isn't that bad. Take it easy on the boy. Don't worry.

Grammatical Structures

Tenses: simple present, present
continuous, future (be going
to);
Verb BE and other verbs
(affirmative and negative);
Imperatives (affirmative and
negative);
Modal (can't);
Verbs (hate to, have to, like to,
need to, want to)

Expressions

He's a pain in the neck.
I've got to get up.
I'll ask him to the dance.
I'll think about it.
What's the matter?

Grammatical Structures

Tenses: simple present, past,
present and past continuous,
future (be going to, will);
Frequency adverbs;
Modal (can't);
Infinitive of purpose;
Comparative of adjective
(good–better);
Verbs (have to, like to, want to)

Expressions

He gets along well with people.
Have a good day.
Sorry I'm late.
I know how you feel.
I wonder what she wants.
He's going to pick her up.
Right away.
What's this I hear?

Grammatical Structures

Tenses: simple present, past, present and past continuous, future;
Intensifier (really);
Modal (can/could, should);
Verb + gerund (enjoy talking);
Adverbial clause (when . . .);
Relative clause (who . . .);
Conditional (would);
Verbs (have to, like to, plan to, want to)

Expressions

I couldn't believe it!
What's the problem?
Wait and see what happens.
Would you like to move?
Are you kidding?
Don't be silly.
It's ridiculous.

Grammatical Structures

Tenses: simple present, past, present and past continuous, future, present perfect;
Modals (can/can't, might, should);
Imperatives;
Imperative + gerund (stop being);
Infinitive of purpose;
Conditional (would/wouldn't);
Comparative of adjective (as . . . as);
Verb + preposition + participle (look forward to seeing);
Adverbial clauses (until . . . / because . . . /before . . . / when . . .);
Verbs (decide to, have to)

Expressions

I can't decide what to do.
That settles it.
Let's get going.
Leave me alone.
Stop being so down.
Cheer up.
We're ready to go.

Grammatical Structures	**Expressions**
Tenses: simple present, past, future;	They hit the books.
Frequency adverbs;	Let's give them time.
Verb + participle (go bicycling, go dancing);	I'm just kidding.
Comparative (better than);	I'm really full.
If clause;	See you soon.
Adverbial clauses (before . . . / when . . . /because . . .);	
Intensifier (too serious);	
Verbs (look forward to, plan to, want to)	

Grammatical Structures	**Expressions**
Tenses: simple present, past, present and past continuous, future;	We look forward to meeting her.
	We have to get going.
	Thanks again for everything.
Present conditional, affirmative and negative (would/wouldn't + simple form of verb);	The rain is really coming down.
	Slow down.
Past conditional, affirmative (wouldn't have + past participle);	Watch out!
	We're on our way.
	Calm down.
Imperatives;	Drop out of school.
Superlative of adjective (fine–one of Canada's finest);	It would have been hard on us.
	I think it's a great idea.
Modals (can/couldn't);	I made it through the year.
Adverbial clauses (when . . . / before . . .)	So long.

INTRODUCTION TO THE TEACHER

Start with Listening: Beginning Comprehension Practice is an audio tape/ text program for beginning level adult and secondary learners of English as a Second Language (ESL). The importance of listening comprehension development in foreign language learning is gaining increased recognition in the field of ESL today. Listening comprehension is viewed, in fact, as the vital ingredient of successful language learning by many (Dunkel, 1986). Today listening is considered the very keystone in the construction of fluency in English.

As Nord (1981) points out, the second language learner must have a much broader competency in listening than in speaking, since the listener has virtually no control over the choice of vocabulary, speech rate, or informational content of the spoken message. As legions of ESL students will attest, they can often read English (if slowly and with the aid of a dictionary), they can do written or spoken manipulations of syntactic patterns (given enough time to think about what they are doing), and they can make themselves understood in survival situations (with the aid of gestures). However, upon encountering English spoken by native speakers, they are often unable to understand what is being said. It is quite likely that such a situation occurs because many ESL students do not receive rigorous training in developing listening skills.

In the past, it was generally assumed that listening skills developed osmotically as students learned to speak English. This audiolingual notion concerning the primacy of speech in language acquisition (especially during the early stages of language learning), is being questioned today by teachers, researchers, and learners. The methodological approach by which students listen in order to learn "how to speak English" is being replaced by a different approach, one in which students listen in order to learn "how to *understand* English." For, as Belasco (1981:19) asserts, it is quite possible to develop so-called 'speaking ability' (vocalizing) and yet be virtually incompetent in understanding the spoken language. The audiotape/text program *Start with Listening* has as its focus listening fluency development. It attempts to help the beginning ESL student to develop listening comprehension of narratives and dialogs in English.

Start with Listening: Beginning Comprehension Practice is a concentrated program of training in listening skill development. The program does not take a shotgun, or multiskill, approach. It does not attempt to teach all skills simultaneously. It is a *listening* course. Some of the exercises do require that the student read directions and take paper-and-pencil tests; some require that the student carry out brief writing tasks; and some ask the student to repeat conversations or to formulate oral responses; however, the major focus of the material is firmly placed on the student's developing listening—rather than reading, writing, or speaking—skills. It is, therefore, anticipated that the student working through *Start with Listening* is receiving instruction in grammar, reading, writing, and conversation simultaneously in a classroom, self-instructional, or tutorial environment.

This program can be used in a classroom setting with a teacher directing the interplay between the tape and the students, or the material can be used in a language laboratory (in a teacher-directed lab or in a library lab). The material might also be used by a student with access to an audiotape cassette player on a self-study basis. If the student has the Tapescript/Answer Key, which is published as a separate volume accompanying the text, she or he can work in an independent, individual, self-instructional mode.

INSTRUCTIONAL DESIGN OF THE LESSONS

Multiple cycles of listening are presented in *Start With Listening*. This approach calls for intense exposure to the language for the beginning student so that she or he can slowly build a depth and breadth of understanding of the narratives and conversations. As Oller (1983) notes, in multiple cycles of listening "the depth of understanding and the range of comprehension increases on each [listening] pass. On the first pass through a text or segment only the bare outlines may be understood. On the second and subsequent passes progress is made from the principal facts of who, what, and where, to the meatier details of when, why, and how, and eventually to presuppositions, associations, and implications. . . . " (p. 18). The multiple cycles of listening include: Cycle I—Narrative (or Conversation); Cycle II—The Narrative in Parts (or The Conversation in Parts); and Cycle III—Narrative Again (or Conversation Again). Comprehension check and listening expansion exercises follow the multiple listening cycles.

Units 1 through 11 contain four lessons each. Lessons 1 and 3 are Narratives; Lessons 2 and 4 are Conversations. Unit 12 contains two more lessons—a third Narrative and a third Conversation.

The format of lessons 1 and 3 is as follows:

A. Narrative

The student listens to the discourse presented in its entirety. The narrator adopts a normal pace of delivery.

B. The Narrative in Parts (Short-Term Memory Practice)

Since it is likely that the student did not understand everything during the first presentation of the narrative, the discourse is segmented into phrases and complete sentences to give the learner the opportunity to go over the information mentally and to absorb the vocabulary and structures used by the narrator.

Psycholinguistic research indicates that memory span for foreign language material is shorter than for native language material (Lado, 1965; Rivers, 1971). One way to help students offset their constricted foreign language memory span is to give them the opportunity to rehearse the information heard, thereby augmenting both their attentional capacity and their overall ability to "chunk" information into phrases and short sentences. This segment of the design provides an opportunity for the non-native speakers to practice short-term memory–expanding procedures in English. During the chunking and rehearsal phase, students become more familiar with the vocabulary and structures used by the narrator.

C. Narrative Again

The student listens to the story once again. Since the student has practiced and reviewed the story in its disassembled form (in The Narrative in Parts), she or he now listens to the story in its original and entire form. Familiarity with the vocabulary and information gleaned from the mental review of the narrative should further increase comprehension of the narrative information during this third listening.

The format of lessons 2 and 4 is as follows:

A. Conversation

A conversation of ever-increasing length and complexity is presented. The thread of the story line involving the main characters weaves a continuous plot throughout the conversations as well as the narratives, but the language of the conversations contains more colloquial and idiomatic expressions than the narrative passages do. Sound effects and illustrations play a prominent role, providing audio and visual context to help students decode the conversations.

B. The Conversation in Parts (Short-Term Memory Practice)

In contrast to engaging in a mental review of the conversation (as in The Narrative in Parts), the student is asked to repeat segments of the conversation. Although the focus of the exercise is on improving aural comprehension, the repetition gives students the opportunity to practice and improve their English pronunciation while they review the content and language used in the conversation.

C. Conversation Again

The conversation is repeated in its entirety once again, placing the individually practiced segments of the discourse back into the conversation's original form.

D. Check Your Comprehension

In both Narrative and Conversation lessons comprehension of information is checked with an objective quiz. The students must listen to the questions. Only the answer choices are written in their texts. Units 11 and 12 contain additional types of objective tests.

E. Varied exercise

In this section varied quizzes expose the learner to a variety of listening test formats (e.g., true/false quizzes, short answer responses, fill-in-the-blanks, dictation, and cloze exercises). These exercises vary in content as well as format, often presenting a novel situation related to the narratives and conversations but not similar to either.

F. Supplementary exercise

Beginning with Unit 6, each unit has a supplementary exercise that requires drawing, describing, identifying, writing, map reading, and figuring. The purpose of these exercises is to offer listening experiences that require the listener to make other than limited choices.

REFERENCES

Belasco, S. 1981. "Aital cal aprene las lengas estrangieras," Comprehension: The key to second language learning. In H. Winitz (ed.), *The Comprehension Approach to Foreign Language Instruction*. Rowley, Mass.: Newbury House Publishers.

Dunkel, P. 1986. Developing listening fluency in L2: Theoretical principles and pedagogical considerations. *The Modern Language Journal*. 70(2):99–106.

Lado, R. 1965. Memory span as a factor in second language learning. *IRAL: International Review of Applied Linguistics in Language Teaching*, 3(2):123–129.

Nord, J.R. 1981. Three steps leading to listening fluency: A beginning. In H. Winitz (ed.), *The Comprehension Approach to Foreign Language Instruction*. Rowley, Mass.: Newbury House Publishers.

Oller, J.W. and Richard-Amato, P. 1983. *Methods That Work: A Smorgasbord of Ideas for Language Teachers*. Rowley, Mass.: Newbury House Publishers.

Rivers, W.M. 1971. Linguistic and psychological factors in speech perception and their implications for teaching materials. In P. Pimsleur and T. Quinn (eds.), *The Psychology of Second Language Learning: Papers from the Second International Congress to Applied Linguistics* (Cambridge, England, September 8–12, 1969.) Cambridge, England: The Cambridge University Press, pp. 123–135. (also Winthrop Publishers, pp. 87–99).

BASIC LESSON FORMAT

A. NARRATIVE

B. THE NARRATIVE IN PARTS —————— phrases and sentences—
                                    listen only

C. NARRATIVE AGAIN

D. CHECK YOUR COMPREHENSION —— multiple choice

E. (VARIOUS EXERCISES) —————— true/false
                                fill-in-the-blanks
                                dictation

A. CONVERSATION

B. THE CONVERSATION IN PARTS —— phrases and sentences—
                                  listen and repeat

C. CONVERSATION AGAIN

D. CHECK YOUR COMPREHENSION —— multiple choice

E. (VARIOUS EXERCISES) —————— true/false
                                fill-in-the-blanks
                                dictation

F. (SUPPLEMENTARY EXERCISES) —— oral responses
                                  listen & draw
                                  listen & describe
                                  listen & recount

ACKNOWLEDGMENTS

The authors would like to acknowledge the help provided and ideas generated by Paula Thompson, Kevin Keating, and Dr. Gary Johnson at the initial stage of program development.

Start With Listening is dedicated to our colleagues and students at The Pennsylvania State University, the University of Arizona, Harvard University, and Georgetown University.

Start With Listening

Beginning Comprehension Practice

Unit

1

1

Sarah Elliot

It's September. Sarah Elliot is at home in San Francisco. It's early in the morning. She's ready to go to the airport. Listen to a story about Sarah.

A. Narrative: Sarah Elliot

B. The Narrative in Parts

Listen to the phrases and sentences. Just listen. Do not repeat.

C. The Narrative Again

Listen and look at the illustration in A. again.

D. Check Your Comprehension

Listen to each question and choose the correct answer from the choices (a) or (b).

1. ____a____   (a) September   (b) November

2. ____b____   (a) at school   (b) at home

3. ____a____   (a) Yes   (b) No

4. ____b____   (a) 16   (b) 18

E. True/False Quiz

Listen to each statement. Is the statement true? Write T on the blank line. Is the statement false (not true)? Write F on the blank line.

1. ____T____

2. ____F____

3. ____F____

4. ____F____

5. ____T____

2

Are You Ready to Go?

Sarah is in her bedroom. Her mother is in the living room. Listen to the conversation between Sarah and her mother.

A. Conversation: Are You Ready to Go?

B. The Conversation in Parts

Listen to the phrases and sentences. Repeat the phrases and sentences after the speaker.

C. The Conversation Again

Listen and look at the illustration in A. again.

D. Check Your Comprehension

Listen to each question and choose the correct answer from the choices (a) or (b).

1. _____a_____   (a) Sarah's mom   (b) Sarah's dad

2. _____b_____   (a) in the bedroom   (b) in the car

3. _____a_____   (a) Yes   (b) No

4. _____a_____   (a) Yes   (b) No

E. True/False Quiz

Listen to each statement. Is the statement true? Write T on the blank line. Is the statement false (not true)? Write F on the blank line.

1. _____T_____

2. _____F_____

3. _____F_____

4. _____T_____

3

The Plane to Boston

Sarah's plane is on the runway. The plane is very large. Listen to a description of the plane.

A. Narrative: The Plane to Boston

B. The Narrative in Parts

Listen to the phrases and sentences. Just listen. Do not repeat.

C. The Narrative Again

Listen and look at the illustration in A. again.

D. Check Your Comprehension

Listen to each question and choose the correct answer from the choices (a) or (b).

1. ____b____   (a) to San Francisco   (b) to Boston

2. ____a____   (a) Yes   (b) No

3. ____b____   (a) at the door   (b) in his seat

4. ____a____   (a) Flight 65   (b) Flight 56

E. True/False Quiz

Listen to each statement. Is the statement true? Write T on the blank line. Is the statement false (not true)? Write F on the blank line.

1. ____F____

2. ____T____

3. ____F____

4. ____T____

5. ____T____

4

Your Ticket, Please

Sarah is in line. The airline agent is very busy. Listen to the conversation between Sarah and the airline agent.

A. Conversation: Your Ticket, Please

B. The Conversation in Parts

Listen to the phrases and sentences. Repeat the phrases and sentences after the speaker.

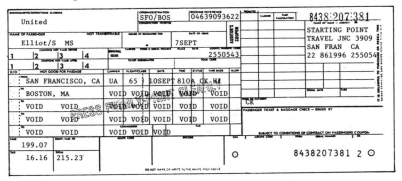

C. The Conversation Again

Listen and look at the illustration in A. again.

D. Check Your Comprehension

Listen to each question and choose the correct answer from the choices (a) or (b).

1. _____*a*_____   (a) in line   (b) on the plane

2. _____*a*_____   (a) Yes   (b) No

3. _____*b*_____   (a) Yes   (b) No

4. _____*b*_____   (a) the flight attendant   (b) the airline agent

E. True/False Quiz

Listen to each statement. Is the statement true? Write T on the blank line. Is the statement false (not true)? Write F on the blank line.

1. ___T___

2. ___F___

3. ___F___

4. ___T___

Unit
$$\overline{\overline{2}}$$

1

On the Plane

Sarah is on the plane to Boston. Tony Rossi is also on the plane. He's from Boston. Listen to a story about Sarah Elliot and Tony Rossi.

A. Narrative: On the Plane

B. The Narrative in Parts

Listen to the phrases and sentences. Just listen. Do not repeat.

C. The Narrative Again

Listen and look at the illustration in A. again.

D. Check Your Comprehension

Listen to each question and choose the correct answer from the choices (a) or (b).

1. ___a___   (a) to Boston   (b) to California

2. ___a___   (a) Yes   (b) No

3. ___b___   (a) California   (b) Boston

4. ___b___   (a) happy   (b) sad

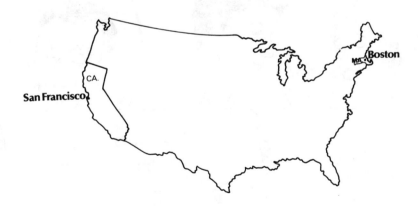

E. True/False Quiz

Listen to each statement. Is the statement true or false? Write T or F on the blank line.

1. ___T___   4. ___T___

2. ___T___   5. ___F___

3. ___T___

2

Where Are You From?

Sarah is next to the window. A businessman is in the aisle seat. Tony Rossi is between Sarah and the businessman. Listen to the conversation between Sarah and Tony.

A. Conversation: Where Are You From?

Where are you from?
Are yo from San Francisco
Yes where are you from
I'm from Boston
Are you student?
Yes I'm student in MIT

B. The Conversation in Parts

Listen to the phrases and sentences. Repeat the phrases and sentences after the speaker.

C. The Conversation Again

Listen and look at the illustration in A. again.

D. Check Your Comprehension

Listen to each question and choose the correct answer from the choices (a) or (b).

1. ____b____   (a) over California   (b) over Arizona

2. ____a____   (a) in the aisle seat   (b) next to the window

3. ____b____   (a) Boston   (b) San Francisco

4. ____a____   (a) MIT   (b) Harvard

5. ____b____   (a) Yes   (b) No

E. True/False Quiz

Listen to each statement. Is the statement true or false? Write T or F on the blank line.

1. __F__

2. __T__

3. __T__

4. __T__

5. __F__

3

On the Harvard Campus

Sarah is at Harvard. She's in front of her dormitory. Listen to a story about Sarah's arrival on campus.

A. Narrative: On the Harvard Campus

B. The Narrative in Parts

Listen to the phrases and sentences. Just listen. Do not repeat.

C. The Narrative Again

Listen and look the illustration in A. again.

D. Check Your Comprehension

Listen to each question and choose the correct answer from the choices (a) or (b).

1. ___b___   (a) inside her dormitory   (b) in front of her dormitory

2. ___b___   (a) tired and sad   (b) tired and happy

3. ___a___   (a) 6:30 in the evening   (b) 6:30 in the morning

4. ___a___   (a) Yes   (b) No

5. ___b___   (a) Yes   (b) No

E. True/False Quiz

Listen to each statement. Is the statement true or false? Write T or F on the blank line.

1. ___T___

2. ___F___

3. ___T___

4. ___F___

5. ___T___

4

We're Roommates

Sarah is at the dormitory. She's at the superintendent's desk. Listen to Sarah and the superintendent at the front desk.

A. Conversation: We're Roommates

B. The Conversation in Parts

Listen to the phrases and sentences. Repeat the phrases and sentences after the speaker.

C. The Conversation Again

Listen and look at the illustrations in A. again.

D. Check Your Comprehension

Listen to each question and choose the correct answer from the choices (a) or (b).

1. _____a_____   (a) at the front desk   (b) in front of the dormitory

2. _____b_____   (a) Yes   (b) No

3. _____b_____   (a) Room 202   (b) Room 210

4. _____b_____   (a) Sarah's classmate   (b) Sarah's roommate

5. _____a_____   (a) Yes   (b) No

E. True/False Quiz

Listen to each statement. Is the statement true or false? Write T or F on the blank line.

1. _____F_____   4. _____T_____

2. _____F_____   5. _____F_____

3. _____T_____

Unit

3

1

Cristina Santos

Cristina Santos is Sarah's roommate. She's from St. Louis, Missouri. She and her parents moved there from Venezuela last year. She's a new student at Harvard. Listen to a story about Cristina.

A. Narrative: Cristina Santos

B. The Narrative in Parts

Listen to the phrases and sentences. Just listen. Do not repeat.

C. The Narrative Again

Listen and look at the illustration in A. again.

D. Check Your Comprehension

Listen to each question and choose the correct answer from the choices (a) or (b).

1. _____a_____   (a) St. Louis   (b) San Francisco

2. _____b_____   (a) unfriendly   (b) friendly

3. _____d_____   (b) brown   (b) blue

4. _____b_____   (a) 4' 5"   (b) 5' 2"

5. _____a_____   (a) Yes   (b) No

E. Yes/No Quiz

Listen to each statement about Cristina. Is the statement correct? Put a circle around *Yes*. Is the statement incorrect (not correct)? Put a circle around *No*.

1. (Yes)   No   4. Yes   (No)

2. Yes   (No)   5. (Yes)   No

3. Yes   (No)   6. (Yes)   No

2

There's a Party Tonight

It's a Saturday night in October. Sarah and Cristina are in their dormitory room. Cristina is on the phone. Listen to Cristina's conversation about a party tonight.

A. Conversation: There's a Party Tonight

B. The Conversation in Parts

Listen to the phrases and sentences. Repeat the phrases and sentences after the speaker.

C. The Conversation Again

Listen and look at the illustration in A. again.

D. Check Your Comprehension

Listen to each question and choose the correct answer from the choices (a) or (b).

1. ___b___   (a) at a party   (b) in the dormitory

2. ___b___   (a) Sunday night   (b) Saturday night

3. ___a___   (a) at Paul's house   (b) at Tony's house

4. ___a___   (b) to a movie   (b) to a party

5. ___a___   (a) Tony   (b) Cristina

E. True/False Quiz

Listen to each statement. Is the statement true or false? Write T or F on the blank line.

1. ___F___

2. ___T___

3. ___F___

4. ___T___

5. ___T___

3

A Serious Student

Sarah is very studious. She's very serious about her studies. She's often in the language lab late at night. Listen to a story about Sarah's studies.

A. Narrative: A Serious Student

B. The Narrative in Parts

Listen to the phrases and sentences. Just listen. Do not repeat.

```
                        Harvard University
                      Office of the Registrar
                    Faculty of Arts & Sciences
                          Course Report

    Sarah Elliot              HOF                  FC    SEPT 14

    No Concentration                                          FR

       COURSE
    PSYCH 1                 0.5  Fall Course
    ENGLISH 10              0.5  Fall Course
    HIS-EUR-STD A-13        0.5  Fall Course
    MATH 1a                 0.5  Fall Course
    FRENCH CON              0.5  Fall Course
    PHYS-ED SWIM            0.0  Fall Course
```

C. The Narrative Again

Listen and look at the illustration in A. again.

D. Check Your Comprehension

Listen to each question and choose the correct answer from the choices (a) or (b).

1. ___b___   (a) five   (b) six

2. ___a___   (a) Yes   (b) No

3. ___a___   (a) French   (b) psychology

4. ___a___   (a) French class   (b) English class

5. ___b___   (a) in the afternoon (b) in the evening

E. Yes/No Quiz

Listen to each statement. Is the statement correct or incorrect (not correct)? Circle *Yes* or *No*.

1. (Yes)　　No   4. Yes　　(No)

2. (Yes)　　No   5. (Yes)　　No

3. Yes　　(No)   6. Yes　　(No)

4

How About a Movie Tonight?

It's fall. It's a cold afternoon in early November. It's four o'clock on a Sunday afternoon. Sarah is studying in her room. Listen to Sarah and Tony's conversation on the phone.

A. Conversation: How About a Movie Tonight?

B. The Conversation in Parts

Listen to the phrases and sentences. Repeat the phrases and sentences after the speaker.

C. The Conversation Again

Listen and look at the illustration in A. again.

D. Check Your Comprehension

Listen to each question and choose the correct answer from the choices (a) or (b).

1. ___a___   (a) It's fall.   (b) It's summer.

2. ___a___   (a) studying for a test   (b) eating pizza

3. ___b___   (a) studying for a test   (b) thinking about Sarah

4. ___b___   (a) Yes   (b) No

5. ___b___   (a) to a movie   (b) to French class

E. True/False Quiz

Listen to each statement. Is the statement true or false? Write T or F on the blank line.

1. ___F___

2. ___T___

3. ___F___

4. ___F___

5. ___F___

Unit

4

1

Tony Rossi

Tony Rossi is studying at MIT. He's in his third year at MIT. He's a junior. Listen to a story about Tony.

A. Narrative: Tony Rossi

B. The Narrative in Parts

Listen to the phrases and sentences. Just listen. Do not repeat.

C. The Narrative Again

Listen and look at the illustration in A. again.

D. Check Your Comprehension

Listen to each question and choose the correct answer.

1. _____a_____   (a) a junior   (b) a senior

2. _____b_____   (a) brown   (b) green

3. _____b_____   (a) French   (b) computer science

4. _____a_____   (a) one   (b) two

5. _____b_____   (a) Tony's mother   (b) Tony's father

6. _____a_____   (a) Tony's father   (b) Tony's girlfriend

E. That's Right/That's Wrong Quiz

Listen to each statement about Tony. Is the statement right or wrong? Circle *That's right* or *That's wrong.*

1. That's right.   That's wrong.   5. That's right.   That's wrong.

2. That's right.   That's wrong.   6. That's right.   That's wrong.

3. That's right.   That's wrong.   7. That's right.   That's wrong.

4. That's right.   That's wrong.

2

Sarah's Really Different

Tony's roommate is François Reynard. He's from Montreal, Canada. François is studying at MIT. His major is also computer science. It's November 15th. It's late at night. François and Tony are watching television in their apartment. Listen to their conversation.

A. Conversation: Sarah's Really Different

B. The Conversation in Parts

Listen to the phrases and sentences. Repeat the phrase and sentences after the speaker.

C. The Conversation Again

Listen and look at the illustration in A. again.

D. Check Your Comprehension

Listen to each question and choose the correct answer.

1. __b__ (a) Canada (b) France

2. __a__ (a) computer science (b) French

3. __b__ (a) in their dormitory (b) in their apartment

4. __b__ (a) the beginning (b) the middle

5. __a__ (a) Tony's girlfriend (b) François' girlfriend

E. Yes/No Quiz

What is Tony saying about Sarah? Listen to each statement. Is Tony saying this about Sarah? Put a circle around *Yes*. Is Tony not saying this? Put a circle around *No*.

1. Yes No   4. Yes No

2. Yes No   5. Yes No

3. Yes No   6. Yes No

3

François's Family

François Reynard is Canadian. His home is in Montreal, Canada.
Listen to a story about François's family.

A. Narrative: François's Family.

B. The Narrative in Parts

Listen to the phrases and sentences. Just listen. Do not repeat.

C. The Narrative Again

Listen and look at the illustration again.

D. Check Your Comprehension

Listen to each question and choose the correct answer.

1. __b__   (a) He's French.   (b) He's Canadian.

2. __b__   (a) in Boston   (b) in Montreal

3. __a__   (a) four children   (b) six children

4. __a__   (a) a lawyer   (b) a writer

5. __b__   (a) a lawyer   (b) a writer

6. __a__   (a) two girls   (b) three girls

E. True/False Quiz

Listen to each statement. Is the statement true or false? Write T or F on the blank line.

1. __T__   4. __F__

2. __T__   5. __F__

3. __F__   6. __T__

4

He's Driving Me Crazy

It's a Sunday evening in early December. François's family is eating dinner. The telephone is ringing. François is calling. Listen to the conversation between François and his mother.

A. Conversation: He's Driving Me Crazy

B. The Conversation in Parts

Listen to the phrases and sentences. Repeat the phrases and sentences after the speaker.

C. The Conversation Again

Listen and look at the illustration in A. again.

D. Check Your Comprehension

Listen to each question and choose the correct answer.

1. ___a___   (a) eating dinner   (b) eating breakfast

2. ___a___   (a) his roommate   (b) his girlfriend

3. ___b___   (a) François   (b) François's roommate

4. ___b___   (a) François   (b) François's roommate

5. ___a___   (a) to Montreal   (b) to Boston

6. ___b___   (a) Yes   (b) No

E. True/False Quiz

Listen to each statement. Is the statement true or false? Write T or F on the blank line.

1. ___T___   4. ___T___

2. ___F___   5. ___F___

3. ___F___   6. ___T___

Unit

$$\overline{\underline{5}}$$

1

Sarah Has a Problem

It's 10:30 at night on a Thursday in the middle of December. Sarah's sitting at her desk in the dormitory. Listen to a story about Sarah and her problem.

A. Narrative: Sarah Has a Problem

B. The Narrative in Parts

Listen to the phrases and sentences. Just listen. Do not repeat.

C. The Narrative Again

Listen and look at the illustration in A. again.

D. Check Your Comprehension

Listen to each question and choose the correct answer.

1. _____c_____   (a) on her bed   (b) on the floor   (c) at her desk

2. _____b_____   (a) watching TV   (b) studying for a test   (c) talking to Cristina's friends

3. _____c_____   (a) Cristina   (b) Cristina's friends   (c) Sarah

4. _____b_____   (a) her parents   (b) her test   (c) her boyfriend

5. _____a_____   (a) angry   (b) happy   (c) tired

E. Identifying Quiz

Who is doing these things—Sarah or Cristina? Listen to each question. Write the answer on the blank line.

1. ___Sarah___   4. ___Sarah___

2. ___Cristina___   5. ___Sarah___

3. ___Cristina___

2

I Can't Study

The noise in Sarah's room is driving her crazy. She's talking to Cristina and her friends. Listen to the conversation.

A. Conversation: I Can't Study

B. The Conversation in Parts

Listen to the phrases and sentences. Repeat the phrases and sentences after the speaker.

C. The Conversation Again

Listen and look at the illustration in A. again.

D. Check Your Comprehension

Listen to each question and choose the correct answer.

1. __b__   (a) Julia is talking   (b) The music is   (c) She has a
             to her.   too loud.   headache.

2. __a__   (a) tomorrow   (b) next week   (c) in a few days

3. __c__   (a) a swimming   (b) a French test   (c) a history test
             test

4. __b__   (a) studying for   (b) having a   (c) leaving for a
             a test   party   movie

5. __a__   (a) to a movie   (b) to a party   (c) to a restaurant

E. True/False Quiz

Listen to each statement. Is the statement true? Draw a circle (○) on the blank line. Is the statement false? Draw a square (□) on the blank line.

1. __□__   4. __□__

2. __○__   5. __○__

3. __□__

3

Tony's Part-Time Job

It's lunch time in the cafeteria at Tony's university, MIT. The cafeteria is crowded. Some students are sitting and eating. Other students are getting their food. Tony's working in the cafeteria. Listen to a story about Tony's part-time job in the cafeteria.

A. Narrative: Tony's Part-Time Job

B. The Narrative in Parts

Listen to the phrases and sentences. Just listen. Do not repeat.

C. The Narrative Again

Listen and look at the illustration in A. again.

D. Check Your Comprehension

Listen to each question and choose the correct answer.

1. ____b____   (a) morning   (b) noon   (c) evening

2. ____b____   (a) a weekend job   (b) a part-time job   (c) a full-time job

3. ____c____   (a) washing dishes   (b) sweeping the floor   (c) frying hamburgers

4. ____a____   (a) washing dishes   (b) making french fries   (c) frying hamburgers

5. ____c____   (a) talking to Tony   (b) eating a hamburger   (c) standing in line

6. ____c____   (a) Yes   (b) No   (c) I don't know.

E. That's Right/That's Wrong Quiz

Listen to each statement about Tony and his father. Is the statement true? Put a circle around *That's right*. Is the statement not true? Put a circle around *That's wrong*.

1. That's right.   *(That's wrong.)*   4. That's right.   *(That's wrong.)*

2. *(That's right.)*   That's wrong.   5. *(That's right.)*   That's wrong.

3. That's right.   *(That's wrong.)*   6. *(That's right.)*   That's wrong.

4

Dad, Don't Worry

Tony and his father are sitting at a table in the cafeteria. Tony's father is eating his lunch. He has two big hamburgers and a piece of apple pie on his tray. Tony is drinking a cup of coffee. Tony's on a coffee break. Tony and his father are talking. Listen to their conversation.

A. Conversation: Dad, Don't Worry

B. The Conversation in Parts

Listen to the phrases and sentences. Repeat the phrases and sentences after the speaker.

C. The Conversation Again

Listen and look at the illustration in A. again.

D. Check Your Comprehension

Listen to each question and choose the correct answer.

1. ___c___ (a) at home (b) in a restaurant (c) in the cafeteria

2. ___a___ (a) Yes (b) No (c) I don't know.

3. ___b___ (a) a cup of coffee (b) two hamburgers and a piece of apple pie (c) a hamburger and french fries

4. ___c___ (a) his parents (b) his roommate (c) his girlfriend

5. ___b___ (a) tomorrow (b) No (c) in a year

6. ___a___ (a) Yes (b) No (c) I don't know.

E. Listening Dictation

Listen to each sentence and fill in the missing word.

1. We're a little ___worried___ about you.

2. You're never home on ___weekend___ .

3. I'm ___busy___ during the week.

4. We're going to ___finish___ school.

5. ___Think___ carefully about it.

6. You're both very ___young___ .

Unit

$$\overline{\overline{6}}$$

1

The Elliots:
A Working Couple

Ana and Dave Elliot are Sarah's parents. Ana was born in Colombia, but she and Dave were students together in California. Ana and Dave live in San Francisco, California, with their two sons. Listen to a story about Sarah's parents.

A. Narrative: The Elliots: A Working Couple

B. The Narrative in Parts

Listen to the phrases and sentences. Just listen. Do not repeat.

C. The Narrative Again

Listen and look at the illustrations in A. again.

D. Check Your Comprehension

Listen to each question and choose the correct answer.

1. ___c___   (a) in a bank   (b) at home   (c) in San Francisco

2. ___b___   (a) Dave   (b) Ana   (c) the Elliots

3. ___a___   (a) Dave   (b) Ana   (c) Sarah

4. ___a___   (a) Yes   (b) No   (c) Maybe

5. ___b___   (a) in the   (b) after work   (c) on Sundays
                    afternoon

E. True/False Quiz

Listen to each statement. Is the statement true or false? Write T or F on the blank line.

1. ___T___

2. ___F___

3. ___F___

4. ___F___

5. ___T___

6. ___T___

7. ___F___

2

What a Day!

It's a Friday evening in January at the Elliots' home. Dave is home from work. He's in the living room watching TV. The boys are not home. Ana is coming in the door.

A. Conversation: What a Day!

B. The Conversation in Parts

Listen to the phrases and sentences. Repeat the phrases and sentences after the speaker.

C. The Conversation Again

Listen and look at the illustration in A. again.

D. Check Your Comprehension

Listen to each question and choose the correct answer.

1. _____c_____   (a) upstairs   (b) at work   (c) in the living room

2. _____a_____   (a) watching TV   (b) cooking dinner   (c) I don't know.

3. _____b_____   (a) Yes   (b) No   (c) Maybe

4. _____c_____   (a) a cold drink   (b) water   (c) tea

5. _____c_____   (a) at the bank   (b) at home   (c) at a restaurant

E. True/False Quiz

Listen to each statement. Is the statement true or false? Write T or F on the blank line.

1. ___T___   4. ___T___

2. ___F___   5. ___F___

3. ___F___   6. ___T___

3

The Boys Are Different

Ana and Dave are sitting at a table in the Japanese restaurant. They're waiting for their dinner. They're drinking tea and talking about their children, Jason and Eric.

A. Narrative: The Boys Are Different

B. The Narrative in Parts

Listen to the phrases and sentences. Just listen. Do not repeat.

C. The Narrative Again

Listen and look at the illustration in A. again.

D. Check Your Comprehension

Listen to each question and choose the correct answer.

1. ___b___   (a) Yes   (b) No   (c) Maybe

2. ___b___   (a) elementary   (b) high school   (c) college

3. ___a___   (a) Eric   (b) Jason   (c) Dave

4. ___b___   (a) Eric   (b) Jason   (c) Ana

5. ___a___   (a) Jason's school work   (b) Ana's job   (c) Dave's job

E. True/False Quiz

Listen to each statement. Is the statement true or false? Write T or F on the blank line.

1. ___T___

2. ___F___

3. ___T___

4. ___F___

5. ___T___

6. ___F___

F. Listening to Identify

The restaurant is not very crowded. Ana and Dave are at one of the tables. Listen to a description of some people in the restaurant. Put a number on each person. Ready?

4

Don't Worry So Much

Ana and Dave are enjoying their Japanese meal. Ana's eating shrimp tempura, and Dave is having sushi. The food is delicious. Listen to the conversation at dinner.

A. Conversation: Don't Worry So Much

B. The Conversation in Parts

Listen to the phrases and sentences. Repeat the phrases and sentences after the speaker.

C. The Conversation Again

Listen and look at the illustration in A. again.

D. Check Your Comprehension

Listen to each question and choose the correct answer.

1. ___c___   (a) Chinese   (b) Italian   (c) Japanese

2. ___b___   (a) at school   (b) in his room   (c) in the
                                                          living room

3. ___c___   (a) baseball   (b) basketball   (c) soccer

4. ___a___   (a) get into   (b) do his   (c) work at his
                  trouble   homework   computer

5. ___b___   (a) He's smart.   (b) He's   (c) He's bad.
                                     good-looking.

E. True/False Quiz

Listen to each statement. Is the statement true or false? Write T or F on the blank line.

1. _____   5. ___T___

2. ___F___   6. ___T___

3. ___F___   7. ___F___

4. ___T___

F. Listening To Complete the Picture

This is a picture of an Italian restaurant. The artist didn't finish the picture. You can complete it. Listen to a description of the things and people in this restaurant. Have your pencil ready.

Unit

$$\overline{\overline{7}}$$

1

Jason Is a Pain in the Neck

It's a Monday evening in late January. Eric's in his bedroom. He's trying to study. He can't study very well. Jason's playing his stereo. The music is loud. Eric is thinking about his brother. Listen.

A. Narrative: Jason Is a Pain in the Neck

B. The Narrative in Parts

Listen to the phrases and sentences. Just listen. Do not repeat.

C. The Narrative Again

Listen and look at the illustration in A. again.

D. Check Your Comprehension

Listen to each question and choose the correct answer.

1. ___b___   (a) listen to music   (b) study   (c) sleep

2. ___b___   (a) happy   (b) unhappy   (c) sick

3. ___a___   (a) not very much   (b) a lot   (c) very much

4. ___a___   (a) talks on the   (b) smokes   (c) eats too
                    telephone   cigarettes   much

5. ___a___   (a) a battery   (b) a girlfriend   (c) a radio

6. ___b___   (a) a car   (b) more money   (c) a brother

7. ___b___   (a) before his test   (b) after his test   (c) during his
                                                           test

E. Identifying Quiz

Listen to six statements about Eric or Jason. Who is the statement about? Touch the picture of Eric or Jason. *Example*: You will hear: Jason likes to play loud music. Touch Jason's picture. Ready?

2

Eric, You Study Too Much

Eric is studying and Jason is listening to music. The telephone is ringing. Listen to the telephone conversation between Eric and one of his friends.

A. Conversation: Eric, You Study Too Much

B. The Conversation in Parts

Listen to the phrases and sentences. Repeat the phrases and sentences after the speaker.

C. The Conversation Again

Listen and look at the illustration again.

D. Check Your Comprehension

Listen to each question and choose the correct answer.

1. ___c___   (a) Jason   (b) Bill   (c) Susan

2. ___a___   (a) Yes   (b) No   (c) Maybe

3. ___c___   (a) go to school   (b) go to a movie   (c) go to a dance

4. ___a___   (a) Jason's taking   (b) Susan is going   (c) neither (a)
              a test.   to a dance.   nor (b)

5. ___a___   (a) Eddie   (b) Eric   (c) Jason

6. ___a___   (a) upset   (b) happy   (c) nervous

7. _____   (a)   (b)   (c)

E. True/False Quiz

Listen to five statements about Eric. Is the statement true? Shake your head *Yes* (up and down). Is the statement false? Shake your head *No* (side to side).

3

Jason Is Smart, But . . . .

Jason is lying on his bed. He isn't sleeping. He's thinking about his report card. He's worried about something. What is Jason worried about? Listen.

A. Narrative: Jason Is Smart, But . . . .

B. The Narrative in Parts

Listen to the phrases and sentences. Just listen. Do not repeat.

C. The Narrative Again

Listen and look at the illustration in A. again.

D. Check Your Comprehension

Listen to each question and choose the correct answer.

1. ___*a*___   (a) Yes   (b) No   (c) I don't know.

2. ___*a*___   (a) Yes   (b) No   (c) I don't know.

3. ___*b*___   (a) Yes   (b) No   (c) I don't know.

4. ___*a*___   (a) Yes   (b) No   (c) I don't know.

5. ___*c*___   (a) Yes   (b) No   (c) I don't know.

6. ___*c*___   (a) Yes   (b) No   (c) I don't know.

E. Listening Dictation

You will hear the sentence at normal speed. Just listen. You will then hear the sentence in phrases. Write all the phrases. You will hear the sentence again at normal speed. Check your work.

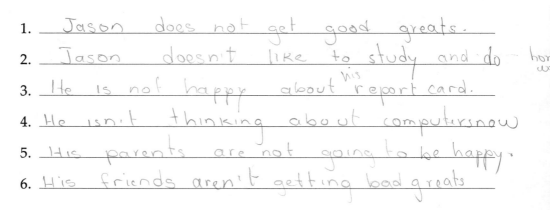

1. Jason does not get good greats.

2. Jason doesn't like to study and do hom wo

3. He is not happy about his report card.

4. He isn't thinking about computirsnow

5. His parents are not going to be happy.

6. His friends aren't getting bad greats

4

A D in Biology!

Jason wants to talk to Eric. He leaves his room. He knocks on Eric's bedroom door. Eric opens his door. Listen.

A. Conversation: A D in Biology!

B. The Conversation in Parts

Listen to the phrases and sentences. Repeat the phrases and sentences after the speaker.

C. The Conversation Again

Listen and look at the illustration in A. again.

D. Check Your Comprehension

Listen to each question and choose the correct answer.

1. ___c___ (a) Who are you? (b) Where are Mom and Dad?

    (c) What do you want?

2. ___a___ (a) A   (b) B   (c) C

3. ___c___ (a) A   (b) B   (c) neither A nor B

4. ___b___ (a) go to college (b) join the navy (c) teach biology

5. ___c___ (a) his mother   (b) his father   (c) his brother

E. Identifying Feelings

Listen to the speaker. Is the speaker happy, sad, angry, or nervous? Is the speaker happy? Put an X next to the word *happy*. Is the speaker sad? Put an X next to the word *sad*. Is the speaker nervous? Put an X next to the word *nervous*. Is the speaker angry? Put an X next to the word *angry*.

1. ___✕___ happy _____ sad _____ nervous _____ angry

2. _____ happy ___✕___ sad _____ nervous _____ angry

3. _____ happy ___✕___ sad _____ nervous _____ angry

4. _____ happy _____ sad _____ nervous ___✕___ angry

5. _____ happy _____ sad _____ nervous ___✕___ angry

6. _____ happy _____ sad ___✕___ nervous _____ angry

7. ___✕___ happy _____ sad _____ nervous _____ angry

F. Listen and Write the Grades

Sumiko is one of Jason's friends. Here is her report card. Is she a good student? Let's see. Listen carefully and fill out Sumiko's report card.

Name	Sumiko Mori	Semester	Fall
School	Wagner High School	Adviser	Miss Nelson

Subject	Grade
Art	A
Chemistry	A
English	C
Geometry	A
German	D
History	B
Physical Education	A

Total Number of Days Absent ___0___

Total Number of Days Late ___5___

Unit

8

1

Dave's Job and Interests

It's a Friday morning in the Elliot house. The boys are eating their breakfast. Ana's getting ready to leave for work. Dave is also getting ready to leave for the office. Listen to a story about Dave Elliot's work and his interests.

A. Narrative: Dave's Job and Interests

B. The Narrative in Parts

Listen to the phrases and sentences. Just listen. Do not repeat.

C. The Narrative Again

Listen and look at the illustration in A. again.

D. Check Your Comprehension

Listen to each question and choose the correct answer.

1. He's in his _____ 40s.

   ___b___   (a) early   (b) mid   (c) late

2. ___a___   (a) Yes   (b) No   (c) I don't know.

3. ___a___   (a) tennis   (b) basketball   (c) football

4. ___b___   (a) on Mondays (b) on Saturdays   (c) on Sundays

5. ___b___   (a) Yes   (b) No   (c) I don't know.

6. ___b___   (a) always   (b) sometimes   (c) never

E. True/False Quiz

Listen to six statements. Is the statement correct? Raise your right hand. Is the statement incorrect (not correct)? Raise your left hand.

2

Your Daughter Called

Dave's office is on the 12th floor of a large, modern office building in downtown San Francisco. He's just getting off the elevator and walking quickly toward his office. Dave is a half-hour late for work this morning. Listen to the conversation between Dave and his secretary, Pamela.

A. Conversation: Your Daughter Called

B. The Conversation in Parts

Listen to the phrases and sentences. Repeat the phrases and sentences after the speaker.

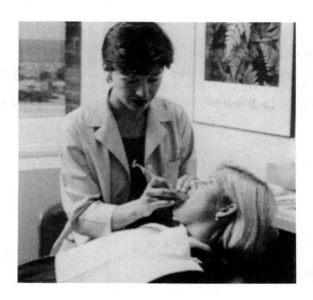

C. The Conversation Again

Listen and look at the illustration in A. again.

D. Check Your Comprehension

Listen to each question and choose the correct answer.

1. _____b_____ (a) Mr. Jones (b) Sorry I'm late. (c) The dentist
                    called.   called.

2. It's in the _____ afternoon.

   _____c_____ (a) early (b) mid (c) late

3. _____b_____ (a) Yes (b) No (c) I don't know.

4. _____c_____ (a) sad (b) sorry (c) surprised

5. _____b_____ (a) last night (b) this evening (c) tomorrow
                                                      morning

6. _____b_____ (a) Yes (b) No (c) Maybe

E. Agree/Disagree Quiz

Listen to five statements about the conversation. Do you agree? Circle the word *Agree*. Do you disagree (not agree)? Circle the word *Disagree*.

1. Agree   Disagree

2. Agree   Disagree

3. Agree   Disagree

4. Agree   Disagree

5. Agree   Disagree

3

Waiting for Sarah to Call Home

It's after dinner at the Elliots'. Eric and Jason are going out. Dave and Ana are staying home tonight. They're waiting for Sarah to call home. Dave and Ana are a little nervous. Listen.

A. Narrative: Waiting for Sarah to Call Home

B. The Narrative in Parts

Listen to the phrases and sentences. Just listen. Do not repeat.

C. The Narrative Again

Listen and look at the illustration in A. again.

D. Check Your Comprehension

Listen to each question and choose the correct answer.

1. ___c___ (a) studying (b) watching TV (c) going out

2. ___a___ (a) Annette (b) Ana (c) Sarah

3. ___c___ (a) a movie (b) a concert (c) the news

4. ___b___ (a) angry (b) worried (c) sad

5. ___c___ (a) books (b) food (c) money

6. ___a___ (a) her father (b) her mother (c) their mother

E. Listening and Identifying Quiz

Look at the picture of Ana and Dave's living room. Listen to the names of objects and pieces of furniture. Is the object or piece of furniture in the living room? Circle *Yes*. Is the object or piece of furniture missing? Circle *No*. Ready?

1. (Yes)   No   5. Yes   (No)

2. (Yes)   No   6. (Yes)   No

3. Yes   (No)   7. (Yes)   No

4. Yes   No

4

I Called to Tell You the Good News!

The phone is ringing. Ana picks up the telephone. It's Sarah. Why is she calling? Listen.

A. Conversation: I Called to Tell You the Good News!

B. The Conversation in Parts

Listen to the phrases and sentences. Repeat the phrases and sentences after the speaker.

C. The Conversation Again

Listen and look at the illustration in A. again.

D. Check Your Comprehension

Listen to each question and choose the correct answer.

1. _____a_____   (a) Yes   (b) No   (c) Maybe

2. _____a_____   (a) Yes   (b) No   (c) Maybe

3. _____a_____   (a) He's doing better in school.

   (b) He's at a friend's house.

   (c) He's watching TV.

4. _____c_____   (a) He has an exam tomorrow.

   (b) He's on a date with Annette.

   (c) He helps Jason with his homework.

5. _____c_____   (a) She's doing well in school.

   (b) She's got a new boyfriend.

   (c) She's engaged to be married.

6. _____b_____   (a) Definitely   (b) Absolutely not   (c) Maybe

7. _____b_____   (a) Yes   (b) No   (c) I don't know.

8. _____a_____   (a) surprised and upset

   (b) happy and excited

   (c) shocked and sad

E. True/False Quiz

Listen to each statement. Is the statement true or false? Write T or F on the blank line.

1. ___T___   4. ___T___

2. ___F___   5. ___F___

3. ___T___   6. ___T___

F. In Love or Breaking Up?

You will hear six conversations. In each conversation, a man and a woman are talking. Listen to their voices and the words they use. Are they in love or are they breaking up? Circle *In love* or *Breaking up*.

1. (In love)   Breaking up

2. (In love)   Breaking up

3. In love   (Breaking up)

4. In love   (Breaking up)

5. (In love)   Breaking up

6. In love   (Breaking up)

Unit

$$9$$

1

Ana's Job and Interests

Ana Elliot works for a large bank. She's the manager of the Personnel
Department. She works with a lot of people every day. What does she
do at work? What does she do after work? Listen.

A. Narrative: Ana's Job and Interests

B. The Narrative in Parts

Listen to the phrases and sentences. Just listen. Do not repeat.

C. The Narrative Again

Listen and look at the illustrations in A. again.

D. Check Your Comprehension

Listen to each question and choose the best answer.

1. _____   (a) Yes   (b) No   (c) I don't know.

2. _____   (a) She fires the worker.

                    (b) She paints beautiful pictures.

                    (c) She chooses the best person for the job.

3. _____   Because

                    (a) Ana talks to many people.

                    (b) the bank needs a new worker.

                    (c) the worker isn't doing a good job.

4. _____   (a) her job

                    (b) quiet activities

                    (c) all kinds of people

5. _____   (a) ones of the ocean

                    (b) ones of the beaches

                    (c) both (a) and (b)

6. _____   (a) She likes to be with her family.

                    (b) She doesn't like to be alone.

                    (c) She works at the bank.

E. Deciding: Is This Ana's Job or Is It Her Interest?

Listen to each statement. Is it Ana's job or Ana's interest? Put a J or an I on the blank line.

1. _____   4. _____

2. _____   5. _____

3. _____   6. _____

2

Leave San Francisco? Are You Kidding?

It's 12:30 P.M. Ana is having lunch in the bank cafeteria with Lee Chan. Lee Chan is the manager of the Loan Department at the bank. Ana and Lee are old friends. Lee tells Ana something very interesting. Listen.

A. Conversation: Leave San Francisco? Are You Kidding?

B. The Conversation in Parts

Listen to the phrases and sentences. Repeat the phrases and sentences after the speaker.

C. The Conversation Again

Listen and look at the illustration in A. again.

D. Check Your Comprehension

Listen to each question and choose the best answer.

1. _____
    (a) Sarah's conversation with Dave.

    (b) Lee's problems on the job.

    (c) Ana's job at the bank.

2. _____
    (a) Yes   (b) No   (c) I don't know.

3. _____
    (a) Yes   (b) No   (c) I don't know.

4. _____
    (a) 19   (b) 24   (c) I don't know.

5. _____
    (a) Tony is there.

    (b) There's a job there.

    (c) He likes the city.

6. _____
    (a) in New York

    (b) in San Francisco

    (c) in Boston

E. True/False Quiz

Listen to each statement. Is the statement true or false? Write T or F on the blank line.

1. _____   4. _____

2. _____   5. _____

3. _____   6. _____

3

Hmmm ... Manager of the Personnel Department ....

When Ana returns to the office from lunch, there is a piece of paper on her desk. It's an announcement of the job opening in the main office of the bank. Ana sits down and reads the announcement. Then she starts to think about her conversation with Lee at lunch. Listen to Ana's thoughts.

A. Narrative: Hmmm . . . Manager of the Personnel Department . . . .

B. The Narrative in Parts

Listen to the phrases and sentences. Just listen. Do not repeat.

NATIONAL TRUST BANKS OF AMERICA

Announcement of Position Opening   *Date: November 10*

TITLE:	Personnel Manager, Main Office
DEPARTMENT:	Personnel
LOCATION:	New York
JOB DUTIES:	Manages staff of 25 employees who are responsible for all personnel files for the NATIONAL TRUST BANKS OF AMERICA main and branch offices. The department collects annual reviews of all employees' work performance. The personnel manager, together with branch office managers, determines compensation increases. The manager works with department managers in the New York office to provide candidates for job vacancies, considering all bank employees as candidates for promotion, within the New York office and among the various branches.
REQUIRED BACKGROUND:	At least ten years' experience in bank personnel management. College degree, preferably relating to the banking industry. Excellent interpersonal skills.

C. The Narrative Again

Listen and look at the illustrations in A. again.

D. Check Your Comprehension

Listen to each question and choose the best answer.

1. _____ (a) a job   (b) an announcement   (c) her lunch

2. _____ (a) Yes   (b) No   (c) I don't know.

3. _____ (a) Lee   (b) Dave   (c) Mr. Smith

4. _____ (a) 40   (b) 50   (c) I don't know.

5. _____ (a) Ana's boys   (b) Ana's workers   (c) Ana's boss

6. _____ (a) their friends   (b) their parents   (c) their grandparents

E. What's Ana Thinking About?
Who's Ana Thinking About?

Ana's thinking about many things—people, places, and things. Write down what or who Ana's thinking about. The list of words will help you spell the words correctly.

New York   promotion   her boss   Lee

Ana's parents $50,000.00   San Francisco

1. _____   4. _____

2. _____   5. _____

3. _____

4

Leave San Francisco? Impossible!

It's early Saturday evening. Ana and Dave are walking along the beach. There are only a few people on the beach. Dave and Ana can see the Golden Gate Bridge in the distance. The sun is setting. Ana tells Dave about the job in New York. Does Dave like the idea? Listen.

A. Conversation: Leave San Francisco? Impossible!

B. The Conversation in Parts

Listen to the phrases and sentences. Repeat the phrases and sentences after the speaker.

C. The Conversation Again

Listen and look at the illustration in A. again.

D. Check Your Comprehension

Listen to each question and choose the best answer.

1. _____ (a) the bridge   (b) the sunset   (c) both (a) and (b)

2. _____ (a) Yes   (b) No   (c) I don't know.

3. _____ (a) Yes   (b) No   (c) I don't know.

4. _____ Because of

   (a) their friends   (b) Ana's parents   (c) both (a) and (b)

5. _____ (a) Probably   (b) Probably not   (c) Definitely not

E. True/False Quiz

Listen to each statement. Is the statement true or false? Write T or F on the blank line.

1. _____   4. _____

2. _____   5. _____

3. _____

F. Leave New York? Impossible!

This is a picture of the Brooklyn Bridge in New York. The sun is setting. The couple is looking at the river. The man in the picture is going to be transferred to a new job in Los Angeles. The couple is sad. They were born in New York City. They love New York. There are some things missing in the picture. What is the couple looking at? Listen and draw the missing things.

Unit

$$\overline{\overline{\textbf{10}}}$$

1

To Tell You the Truth, I Can't Decide What to Do

Ana's writing a letter to Sarah. She's telling her about the job offer in New York. Listen to Ana's letter.

A. Narrative: To Tell You the Truth, I Can't Decide What to Do

B. The Narrative in Parts

Listen to the phrases and sentences. Just listen. Do not repeat.

C. The Narrative Again

Listen and look at the illustration in A. again.

D. Check Your Comprehension

Listen to each question and choose the best answer.

1. _____ (a) She is standing up.

   (b) She is sitting down.

   (c) She is lying down.

2. _____ (a) a week ago (b) a few days ago (c) a year ago

3. _____ (a) a week ago (b) next year (c) immediately

4. _____ (a) Mr. Smith (b) Lee (c) Ana's family

5. _____ (a) It's wonderful. (b) It's too difficult. (c) It's bad.

6. _____ (a) Yes (b) No (c) I don't know.

7. _____ (a) Yes (b) No (c) I don't know.

E. Feelings: Who Thinks This?

Ana   Dave   the boys   Sarah   Eric

Jason   Ana's parents   Mr. Smith

Listen to the phrases and statements about feelings. Who has this feeling? Write the name of the person or persons on the blank line. You may use more than one person in your answer.

1. _____   5. _____

2. _____   6. _____

3. _____   7. _____

4. _____

2

That Settles It!

It's Sunday evening at the Elliots'. Ana and Dave are watching a movie on TV. They're waiting for Sarah's telephone call. The phone suddenly rings.

A. Conversation: That Settles It!

B. The Conversation in Parts

Listen to the phrases and sentences. Repeat the phrases and sentences after the speaker.

C. The Conversation Again

Listen and look at the illustration in A. again.

D. Check Your Comprehension

Listen to each question and choose the best answer.

1. _____   (a) Dave   (b) Sarah   (c) Ana

2. _____   (a) a letter   (b) a job   (c) a problem

3. _____   (a) "What's the problem?"

                    (b) "Well, that settles it!"

                    (c) "I don't know what to do."

4. _____   (a) He likes his job.

                    (b) He has a new girlfriend

                    (c) He doesn't like big cities.

5. _____   (a) next month

                    (b) during the week

                    (c) on weekends

6. _____   (a) "I'll call you next week."

                    (b) "From New York City?"

                    (c) "How's Tony?"

E. Complete the Conversation

After Sarah talks to her mother, she calls Tony. You will hear Sarah's part of the conversation. What does Tony say? Use your own words to speak for Tony.

Tony:

Sarah: Hi, Tony. It's me. I just talked to Mom and Dad.

Tony:

Sarah: They're fine.

Tony:

Sarah: Dad thinks she should take the job. He's not happy about leaving California, but he'll like New York.

Tony:

Sarah: No, he's never been to New York. He's a true Californian. He thinks he hates New York.

Tony:

Sarah: Yes. He was in Boston a long time ago. He liked the city a lot.

Tony:

Sarah: No. He went to college in Los Angeles. UCLA.

Tony:

Sarah: Eric and Jason are fine.

Tony:

Sarah: All right. Go study. I have an exam tomorrow, too. I'll call you tomorrow night.

Tony:

Sarah: Bye, Love.

3

Ana and Dave Make
the Decision

Ana and Dave made a big decision after they talked to Sarah by
phone. What did they decide to do about moving to New York? Listen.

A. Narrative: Ana and Dave Make the Decision

B. The Narrative in Parts

Listen to the phrases and sentences. Just listen. Do not repeat.

C. The Narrative Again

Listen and look at the illustration in A. again.

D. Check Your Comprehension

Listen to each question and choose the best answer.

1. _____ (a) very long   (b) not very long   (c) I don't know.

2. _____ (a) the good things

              (b) the bad things

              (c) both (a) and (b)

3. _____ (a) New York   (b) San Francisco   (c) Boston

4. _____ (a) angry   (b) happy   (c) surprised

5. _____ (a) Dave   (b) Ana   (c) Jason

6. _____ (a) excited   (b) angry   (c) nervous

7. _____ (a) to find a new job

              (b) to celebrate

              (c) to meet some friends

E. Fill In the Blanks

Listen to each statement and fill in the missing words. You will hear each sentence two times. Watch your spelling.

1. Ana and Dave talked for ____ _____ _____ after they spoke to Sarah.

2. They made the _____ to move to New York.

3. Jason was a little _____ when he heard the news.

4. He had many, many _____ to ask.

5. The family went to a _____ for dinner.

6. The move to New York will be a big _____ for everyone.

4

New York's Not the End of the World

The Elliot family is going out to dinner tonight. Eric is telling Jason to hurry up and get ready to leave. Listen to the boys' conversation.

A. Conversation: New York's Not the End of the World

B. The Conversation in Parts

Listen to the phrases and sentences. Repeat the phrases and sentences after the speaker.

C. The Conversation Again

Listen and look at the illustration in A. again.

D. Check Your Comprehension

Listen to each question and choose the best answer.

1. _____   (a) Dave   (b) Ana   (c) Jason

2. _____   (a) Dave   (b) Eric   (c) Jason

3. _____   (a) Eric   (b) Jason   (c) Dave

4. _____   (a) "You'll find new friends."

                (b) "You'll like living in New York."

                (c) "You'll stay with Grandma and Grandpa."

5. _____   (a) Yes   (b) No   (c) Maybe

6. _____   (a) in San Francisco   (b) in New York   (c) both (a) and (b)

E. Eric Said It/Eric Didn't Say It

Listen to each statement. Ask yourself this question. Did Eric say that to Jason? Is your answer "Yes?" Write *Said* on the blank line. Is your answer "No?" Write *Didn't say* on the blank line.

1. _____   5. _____

2. _____   6. _____

3. _____   7. _____

4. _____

F. Figure Out the Check

You will listen to the family order dinner at the restaurant. Put the name and price of each dish on the check.

MENU

The China Wall Restaurant

SOUPS		APPETIZERS	
Egg Drop Soup		Egg Roll	1.25
cup	.75	Fried Shrimp	2.25
bowl	1.50	Fried Chicken Wings	.75

DINNERS

All Dinners Served with Rice.

Chicken

Chicken with Mushrooms 4.75
Chicken with Hot Sauce 5.25

Beef

Beef with Vegetables 3.75
Beef with Chinese Mushrooms 3.50

Duck

Sliced Duck with Vegetables 6.25
House Special Duck 8.00

Seafood

Lobster Cantonese 9.25
Shrimp with Hot Sauce 6.25

CHECK

The China Wall Restaurant

DATE _____

ITEM	COST
TOTAL	
ADD 7% TAX	
GRAND TOTAL	

How much did the meal cost? Look at the menu and figure out the check. Be sure to include the tax.

Unit
11

1

Time for School;
Time for Each Other

It's springtime. Sarah's in the second semester of her freshman year at Harvard. Both she and Tony got good grades last semester. They study a lot, but they also have time for each other. How do they spend their time together? Listen.

A. Narrative: Time for School; Time for Each Other

B. The Narrative in Parts

Listen to the phrases and sentences. Just listen. Do not repeat.

C. The Narrative Again

Listen and look at the illustration in A. again.

D. Check Your Comprehension

You are going to hear six sentences about Tony and Sarah on weekends. Select the correct picture for each activity. For example: The speaker will say, "1. Sometimes Tony and Sarah go bicycling along the Charles River." Find the picture of Tony and Sarah on bicycles along the river. Put a 1 next to the picture. You won't hear about every picture. Be careful. Let's begin.

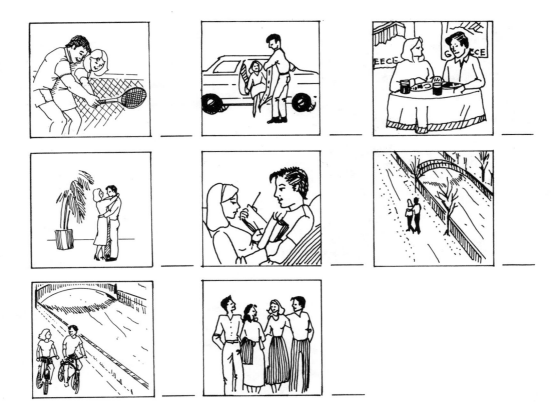

E. Fill In the Blanks

Listen to each statement and fill in the missing words. You will hear each sentence two times.

1. On _____ Tony and Sarah usually don't see each

   other.

2. Sarah is a real _____ .

3. There are quite a few terrific _____ restaurants in

   the Boston area.

4. They ate in a _____ restaurant.

5. During the week, Tony and Sarah _____ _____ _____ .

2

Let's Talk About Something Else

Tony and Sarah are in a small seafood restaurant on Cape Cod. From the window by their table they can see the fishing boats in the harbor. The sun is setting. The sunset is beautiful. Tony and Sarah are not discussing school. What are they talking about? Let's listen.

A. Conversation: Let's Talk About Something Else

B. The Conversation in Parts

Listen to the phrases and sentences. Repeat the phrases and sentences after the speaker.

C. The Conversation Again

Listen and look at the illustration in A. again.

D. Check Your Comprehension

Listen to parts of Tony and Sarah's conversation. What does their tone of voice tell you about their feelings? For example: You will hear Sarah say, "Can you imagine my mother leaving Jason in California!" Sarah does not believe Ana will go to New York without Jason. She is expressing disbelief of the idea. Choose (b) for number 1.

1. _____ (a) happiness (b) disbelief (c) anger

2. _____ (a) happiness (b) disbelief (c) anger

3. _____ (a) worry (b) happiness (c) anger

4. _____ (a) happiness (b) sadness (c) anger

5. _____ (a) fear (b) sadness (c) anger

6. _____ (a) happiness (b) disbelief (c) fear

E. Use a French and English Guidebook

Tony didn't know anything about Montreal so he bought a guide-book of Montreal. The book was in both French and English. There were many interesting pictures in the book. Look at each picture and the French explanation. Then listen to the English explanation and write the English translation under the French.

1. Vieux Montréal _____

Site de choix pour les visiteurs et les Montréalais.

_____

_____

2. Terre des Hommes _____

Une attraction des choix pour les visiteurs et les Montréalais.

_____

_____

3. Beaux Parcs et Jardins

À Montréal on trouve de beaux parcs et jardins.

4. Montréal, Québec, Canada

Montréal Metropolitain a une population de près de 2,500,000 habitants. C'est la deuxième cité du monde quant à sa population de langue français.

3

Leaving for Montreal

It's early Saturday morning. Tony and François are in front of Sarah's dormitory. Tony's putting Sarah's suitcases in the back seat of François's sportscar. Tony's and François's suitcases are already in the trunk. Where are Tony, François, and Sarah going? Listen.

A. Narrative: Leaving for Montreal

Departures ←

B. The Narrative in Parts

Listen to the phrases and sentences. Just listen. Do not repeat.

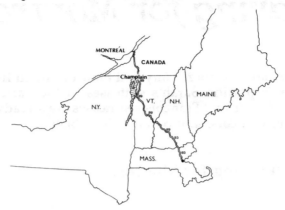

C. The Narrative Again

Listen and look at the illustration in A. again.

D. Check Your Comprehension

Listen to each question and choose the best answer.

1. _____   (a) 93 miles   (b) 320 miles

                 (c) 330 miles   (d) 230 miles

2. _____   (a) by train   (b) by plane

                 (c) by car   (d) by bus

3. _____   Because

                 (a) he's going to Canada

                 (b) he's going to see his parents

                 (c) he's going home with Sarah

                 (d) he's going to take a plane trip

4. _____   (a) to Canada   (b) to Concord

                 (c) to California   (d) to Boston

5. _____
 (a) two weeks (b) one week

     (c) several days (d) one month

6. _____
 (a) southwest (b) southeast

     (c) northeast   (d) northwest

7. _____
 (a) in the morning (b) at noon

     (c) in the evening (d) at midnight

E. Mark the Route to Montreal

Let's go to Montreal with Tony and François. Look at the map. Now listen to the directions, and trace the boys' route on the map.

4

Breakfast at the Reynards'

Tony and François went to bed late Saturday. It's now 10:00 A.M. Sunday morning. The Reynards and Tony are sitting in the kitchen having breakfast. What are they eating? And what are they talking about? Let's listen.

A. Conversation: Breakfast at the Reynards'

B. The Conversation in Parts

Listen to the phrases and sentences. Repeat the phrases and sentences after the speaker.

C. The Conversation Again

Listen and look at the illustrations in A. again.

D. Check Your Comprehension

Listen to each question and choose the best answer.

1. _____   (a) in the kitchen   (b) at a cafeteria

    (c) in the dining room   (d) in the family room

2. _____   (a) the Natural History Museum

    (b) the Museum of Fine Arts

    (c) the Modern Art Museum

    (d) the Geology Museum

3. _____ (a) at the museum   (b) at a restaurant

               (c) at a friend's house   (d) at home

4. _____ (a) after dinner   (b) before lunch

               (c) after breakfast   (d) before dinner

5. _____ (a) She's too serious about him.

               (b) She's too worried about him.

               (c) He's too serious about her.

               (d) He's too old for her.

6. _____ (a) Tony doesn't want a girlfriend.

               (b) François wants a girlfriend.

               (c) François doesn't want a girlfriend

               (d) Sarah wants a boyfriend.

E. Did Tony Say That? Did Sarah Say That?

You will hear seven statements. Did Tony, Sarah, or someone else make the statement? Check the correct choice.

For example: Here's a statement. "Can you imagine my mother leaving Jason in California!"

1. _____ Sarah

     _____ Tony

     _____ Someone else

Sarah said this to Tony. Check "Sarah" for number 1.

2. _____ Sarah

     _____ Tony

     _____ Someone else

3. _____ Sarah

_____ Tony

_____ Someone else

4. _____ Sarah

_____ Tony

_____ Someone else

5. _____ Sarah

_____ Tony

_____ Someone else

6. _____ Sarah

_____ Tony

_____ Someone else

7. _____ Sarah

_____ Tony

_____ Someone else

F. Complete the Conversation

After breakfast with the Reynards, Tony receives a long-distance call from Sarah. You will hear Tony's part of the conversation. What do you think Sarah says? Use your own words to speak for Sarah.

Sarah:

Tony: Fine, thanks, Honey. I'm really happy you called.

Sarah:

Tony: The trip was great, but we were really tired when we arrived last night.

Sarah:

Tony: Yes, we had lunch on the lake about 1:30. The scenery was beautiful.

Sarah:

Tony: I miss you, too, Sarah. But we'll be together again soon—in a week.

Sarah:

Tony: I hope you have a good week, too. See you soon, Sweetheart.

Sarah:

Tony: Bye, Sarah. I love you.

Unit

12

1

Walking Around Downtown Montreal

François and Tony drove to the Museum of Fine Arts. They spent several hours looking at the paintings of Canadian and foreign artists. They didn't spend the whole afternoon at the museum. Where else did the two friends go? Listen.

A. Narrative: Walking Around Downtown Montreal

Museum of Fine Arts

Dominion Square

Notre Dame Church

McGill University

B. The Narrative in Parts

Listen to the phrases and sentences. Just listen. Do not repeat.

C. The Narrative Again

Listen and look at the illustration in A. again.

D. Check Your Comprehension

Listen to each question and choose the best answer.

1. _____   (a) looked at beautiful skyscrapers

   (b) changed their clothes

   (c) looked at paintings

   (d) ate lunch

2. _____   (a) the whole afternoon   (b) the whole day

   (c) a few minutes   (d) a few hours

3. _____   (a) at McGill University

   (b) at Dominion Square

   (c) at the Museum of Fine Arts

   (d) at Le Café de Paris

4. _____   (a) pizza with mushrooms

   (b) French bread and cheese

   (c) a roast beef sandwich

   (d) a hamburger and Coke

5. _____   (a) by subway and car   (b) by bus and car

   (c) by taxi   (d) by streetcar

E. Identify the Sites

Look at the pictures of some of the places Tony and François visited. Listen to the instructions about the pictures. Write the answers.

1.

2.

3.

4.

5.

1. _____   _____

2. _____   _____

3. _____   _____

    _____

4. _____

5. _____

2

Returning to Boston

Tony and François are getting ready to drive back to Boston. They spent a busy week seeing friends and relatives of François and sightseeing in Montreal. They're saying good-bye to François's parents. Listen.

A. Conversation: Returning to Boston

B. The Conversation in Parts

Listen to the phrases and sentences. Repeat the phrases and sentences after the speaker.

C. The Conversation Again

Listen and look at the illustrations in A. again.

D. Check Your Comprehension

Listen to some of the statements you heard in the conversation. Who said these things? Choose the best answer.

1. _____   (a) Tony's mother   (b) François

                 (c) François's mother   (d) Tony

2. _____   (a) Sarah   (b) Tony

                 (c) Tony's mother   (d) François

3. _____   (a) François's mother   (b) François's father

                 (c) Tony   (d) François

4. _____   (a) François   (b) Tony

                     (c) Tony's mother   (d) François's mother

5. _____   (a) Tony   (b) Tony's mother

                     (c) François's mother   (d) François

6. _____   (a) François's father   (b) Tony

                     (c) the bus driver   (d) François

E. Fill In the Blanks

Listen to each statement and fill in the missing words. You will hear each sentence two times.

1. I can't _____ the week went by so

_____ .

2. Come on. We have to _____ _____ .

3. Have a _____ _____ .

4. The rain is really _____ _____ .

5. We're only _____ 65 miles an hour.

6. _____ _____ the brakes!

7. The brakes are _____ !

F. What Do You Think?

What happened to Tony and François? Write a few sentences about them.

_____

_____

_____

_____

_____

_____

_____

Now read your answer to your teacher or to one of your classmates.

3

The 10 O'Clock News

A 10 o'clock report on the radio tells about a fire and a car accident on Highway 89. Listen to the news report.

A. Narrative: The 10 O'Clock News

B. The Narrative in Parts

Listen to the phrases and sentences. Just listen. Do not repeat.

C. The Narrative Again

Listen and look at the illustration in A. again.

D. Check Your Comprehension

Imagine that you are a reporter at the scene of the fire in the public library. You will hear a fact about the fire. Choose the correct question about the fact. Put a checkmark (√) on the line for the correct answer.

For example: The fire started in the basement.

_____ (a) When did the fire start?

_____ (b) How did the fire start?

_____√_____ (c) Where did the fire start?

_____ (d) Why did the fire start?

The correct question that relates to the fact about this statement is (c). Are you ready?

1. _____   (a) Where is the library?

     _____   (b) How did the fire start?

     _____   (c) Who started the fire?

     _____   (d) When did the fire start?

2. _____   (a) How long did the fire burn?

     _____   (b) How did the firemen put the fire out?

     _____   (c) Where did the firemen find the fire?

     _____   (d) Why did the firemen rush to the library?

3. _____   (a) Who will close the library?

     _____   (b) When did the library close?

     _____   (c) Why will the library be closed?

     _____   (d) How long will the library be closed?

4. _____   (a) Why did the car crash?

     _____   (b) Where did the car crash?

     _____   (c) Who crashed into the bus?

     _____   (d) What did the car crash into?

5. _____   (a) What happened to one of the passengers?

     _____   (b) How many passengers in the car were seriously hurt?

     _____   (c) Why was the passenger in the car killed?

     _____   (d) When was the passenger in the car killed?

6. _____   (a) Who was on the bus?

     _____   (b) Where was the bus when it crashed?

     _____   (c) Where are the bus passengers now?

     _____   (d) How many bus passengers are in critical condition?

7. _____   (a) What happened in the library?

   _____   (b) Where did a car accident occur today?

   _____   (c) When will the music begin on the radio station?

   _____   (d) What will the weather be like on the following
                     day?

E. That's Certain/That's a Guess

You will hear 10 statements about the news report. Is the information in each statement in the news report? If you heard the information reported by the newscaster, circle *That's certain*. If you did not hear the information in the newscast, circle *That's a guess*.

For example: "1. It's 10 o'clock in Waterbury, Vermont." The newscaster said this in the news report. Circle *That's certain*.

"2. A man in a yellow jacket started the fire in the library." The newscaster did not say *who* started the fire, so circle *That's a guess*.

1.   That's certain.   That's a guess.

2.   That's certain.   That's a guess.

3.   That's certain.   That's a guess.

4.   That's certain.   That's a guess.

5.   That's certain.   That's a guess.

6.   That's certain.   That's a guess.

7.   That's certain.   That's a guess.

8.   That's certain.   That's a guess.

9.   That's certain.   That's a guess.

10. That's certain.   That's a guess.

4

An Accident?

Mr. and Mrs. Reynard are asleep. It's midnight. The telephone is ringing in the bedroom. Mr. Reynard reaches for the phone.

A. Conversation: An Accident?

B. The Conversation in Parts

Listen to the phrases and sentences. Repeat the phrases and sentences after the speaker.

BURLINGTON —

WATERBURY —

C. The Conversation Again   VERMONT

Listen and look at the illustration in A. again.

D. Check Your Comprehension

Listen to each question and choose the best answer. Put a check mark on the line for the best answer (√).

1. _____   (a) Tony

   _____   (b) François

   _____   (c) Mr. Reynard

   _____   (d) Mrs. Reynard

2. _____   (a) in Canada

   _____   (b) in Boston

   _____   (c) south of Burlington

   _____   (d) on Highway 89

3. _____   (a) "Get the car."

   _____   (b) "Get dressed."

   _____   (c) "Go back to sleep."

   _____   (d) "Call the police."

4. _____   (a) François is alive.

    _____   (b) Tony is not O.K.

    _____   (c) The police are at the hospital.

    _____   (d) Some tourists were injured.

5. _____   (a) Sarah

    _____   (b) François

    _____   (c) Tony's parents

    _____   (d) François's parents

E. True/False Quiz

Listen to each statement. Is the statement true or false? Write T or F on the blank line.

1. _____   6. _____

2. _____   7. _____

3. _____   8. _____

4. _____   9. _____

5. _____   10. _____

5

Life Goes On

Sarah learned of Tony and François's accident from François's parents. François was hurt. Tony hit his head. He is in a coma. He looks like he is asleep.

A. Narrative: Life Goes On

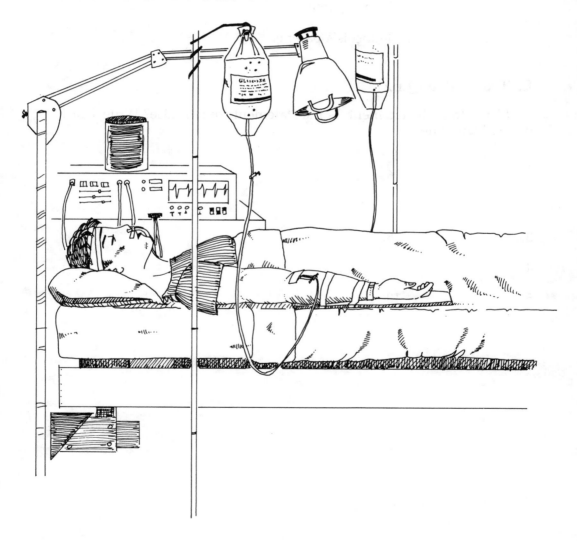

B. The Narrative in Parts

Listen to the phrases and sentences. Just listen. Do not repeat.

C. The Narrative Again

Listen and look at the illustrations in A. again.

D. Check Your Comprehension

Fill in the blanks with the missing words from the narrative. The missing words are similar in meaning to the words in the narrative. They are synonyms. Listen carefully to the new words and write them in the blank spaces. Listen to the paragraphs a second time and check your work.

Sarah was very upset. She couldn't eat for days. She _____

_____ at night. She stopped going to classes.

Tony wouldn't want her _____ school. Sarah

thought about this. Sarah decided _____ in Boston.

She decided _____ her schoolwork.

She _____ to attend classes. She was occupied

with schoolwork during the day. Her friends _____

her to restaurants and movies on weekends. Sarah _____

_____ her first year at the university.

E. Do You Agree? Why Do You Say That?

You will hear 10 statements. Listen to each statement. Do you agree
with the statement? Circle (a), (b), or (c). Then explain in your own
words why you agree, or why you do not agree. In other words, give
your own opinion.

1. (a) I agree.   (b) I don't agree.   (c) I'm not sure.

   Why do you say that? _____

   _____

   _____

2. (a) I agree.   (b) I don't agree.   (c) I'm not sure.

   Why do you say that? _____

   _____

   _____

3. (a) I agree.   (b) I don't agree.   (c) I'm not sure.

   Why do you say that? _____

   _____

   _____

4. (a) I agree.   (b) I don't agree.   (c) I'm not sure.

   Why do you say that? _____

   _____

   _____

5. (a) I agree.   (b) I don't agree.   (c) I'm not sure.

Why do you say that? _____

_____

_____

6. (a) I agree.   (b) I don't agree.   (c) I'm not sure.

Why do you say that? _____

_____

_____

7. (a) I agree.   (b) I don't agree.   (c) I'm not sure.

Why do you say that? _____

_____

_____

8. (a) I agree.   (b) I don't agree.   (c) I'm not sure.

Why do you say that? _____

_____

_____

9. (a) I agree.   (b) I don't agree.   (c) I'm not sure.

Why do you say that? _____

_____

_____

10. (a) I agree.   (b) I don't agree.   (c) I'm not sure.

Why do you say that? _____

_____

_____

6

There's Your Flight, Sarah

Sarah and Cristina are at Logan International Airport in Boston. They're sitting in a coffee shop. They're waiting for Sarah's flight back to California. Cristina's asking Sarah a question. Listen to Cristina's question and Sarah's answer.

A. Conversation: There's Your Flight, Sarah

FLT: →
204
SAN FRANCISCO

B. The Conversation in Parts

Listen to the phrases and sentences. Repeat the phrases and sentences after the speaker.

C. The Conversation Again

Listen and look at the illustration in A. again.

D. Check Your Comprehension

In the conversation, Sarah and Cristina spoke many words to each other, but the conversation was also full of unspoken words and thoughts. You will hear a statement by Sarah or Cristina. On your paper you will read several possible ideas about the statement. Which thoughts come from the words and from what you know about Cristina, Sarah, and their lives?

For example: Sarah says to Cristina, "I didn't want to say good-bye to François. It would be too hard for both of us to do." What does Sarah mean by these words? Does she mean that (a) Sarah doesn't like François? (b) François went to Canada? (c) François is a hard person to be friends with? (d) saying good-bye would make Sarah and François miss Tony? Sarah's words really mean that Sarah and François are so sad about Tony's condition. François feels responsible, and he cares about Tony. It's hard for Sarah and François to see each other without thinking and talking about Tony. You can draw an inference from her words. Sarah did not say, "Saying good-bye would make us both miss Tony," but it is a likely conclusion from all we know about the story. Why is choice (a) not a possible inference? What about choice (b)? What about choice (c)?

Do you think your choice follows from the words and the situation? Write PI for Possible Inference on the blank line for your choice. Stop the tape after each question and explain your answer.

1. _____ (a) François will never dance again.

_____ (b) François will go to California in September.

_____ (c) François will get better and be able to dance again.

_____ (d) François and Cristina will go dancing in September.

2. _____   (a) The Elliots are excited about living in New York.

   _____   (b) The Elliots are leaving California to live near Sarah.

   _____   (c) The Elliots have really enjoyed living in California.

   _____   (d) The Elliots will not like living in New York because the weather is too cold.

3. _____   (a) Cristina helped Sarah finish the school year.

   _____   (b) Cristina helped Sarah after Tony's accident.

   _____   (c) Cristina helped Sarah study for her final exams.

   _____   (d) Cristina helped Sarah by giving her money for her school tuition.

4. _____   (a) Cristina wants Sarah to hurry onto the plane so Cristina can get home before dark.

   _____   (b) Cristina doesn't want people to see her crying.

   _____   (c) Cristina is sad that Sarah is leaving, but she tries to make a joke so they both will not cry.

   _____   (d) Cristina and Sarah will cry if they don't laugh.

E. What Will Happen?

Write the story of Cristina's, Sarah's, Tony's, and François's lives during the coming year. What will happen to each next year? Also, describe what will happen to the Elliots next year. Use your imagination. Write the story out on paper or tell the future of this family and their friends to one of your classmates or to your teacher.

Glossary

GLOSSARY OF
EXPRESSIONS AND IDIOMS

Unit 1

Unit 2

Unit 3

Unit 4

Unit 5

Unit 6

EXERCISE
2A   *What a day*!   It was a busy day.
2A   *What would you like*?   What do you want to drink?
2A   *I'll get it.*   I'll bring it to you.
2A   *Let's not* cook tonight.   I don't want to cook tonight.
2A   *Let's eat out.*   I want to eat at a restaurant with you.
4A   *It isn't that bad.*   It isn't very bad.
4A   *Take it easy on* the boy.   Don't be too demanding on the boy.
4A   *Don't worry.*   There's not a problem.

Unit 7

1A   He's *a pain in the neck.*   He makes me angry sometimes.
2A   *I've got to* get up.   I have to; it's necessary
2A   *I'll ask* him *to* the dance.   I'll invite him to the dance.
2A   *I'll think about it.*   I'll think about this idea.
4A   *What's the matter*?   What's wrong? Is there a problem?

Unit 8

1A   He *gets along* well *with* people.   He likes people and people like him.
1A   *Have a good day.*   I hope you have a nice day.
2A   *Sorry I'm late.*   I'm sorry to be late.
2A   *I know how you feel.*   I understand.
2A   I *wonder what* she *wants.*   I'm not sure what she wants.
3A   He's going to *pick her up.*   He's going to her house to get her.
4A   *Right away*   Immediately
4A   *What's this I hear*?   What are you saying?

Unit 9

2A   *I couldn't believe it*!   I was surprised to hear this.
2A   *What's the problem*?   What's wrong? Is there a problem?
2A   *Wait and see what happens.*   Wait for more information.
2A   *Would you like to move*?   Do you want to live in another town or city?
2A   *Are you kidding*?   Are you joking?
4A   *Don't be silly.*   Don't say that.
4A   *It's ridiculous.*   It's a silly idea.

Unit 10

EXERCISE

1A	I *can't decide what to do.* I don't know what to do.
2A	*That settles it.* Now you know what to do.
4A	*Let's get going.* It's time to leave.
4A	*Leave me alone.* Don't bother me.
4A	*Stop being so down.* Don't feel bad.
4A	*Cheer up.* Be happy.
4A	We're *ready to go.* We can go now.

Unit 11

1A	They *hit the books.* They study very hard.
2A	Let's *give them time.* They need more time.
2A	I'm *just kidding.* I'm not serious.
4A	I'm *really full.* I can't eat any more.
4F	*See you soon.* I'll see you in a short time.

Unit 12

2A	We *look forward to* meeting her. We will be happy to meet her.
2A	We *have to get going.* We have to leave.
2A	*Thanks again for everything.* Thank you again.
2A	*The rain is really coming down.* It's raining very hard.
2A	*Slow down.* Drive more slowly.
2A	*Watch out!* Be careful!
4A	We're *on our way.* We're leaving home now.
4A	*Calm down.* Be quiet. Relax.
5A	*Drop out of school* Leave school
6A	*It would have been hard on us.* It would have been a difficult thing for us to do.
6A	I think *it's a great idea.* It's a wonderful idea.
6A	I *made it through* the year. I finished the year.
6A	*So long.* Goodbye.